D1030749

for the 2-C boys at Gilman School —

The FLAG MAKER

Susan Campbell Bartoletti

BY SUSAN CAMPBELL BARTOLETTI

2004

★

ILLUSTRATED BY CLAIRE A. NIVOLA

Houghton Mifflin Company
Boston 2004

For Stephanie Box, in loving memory of her mother, Peggy
—S.C.B.

For those who grow up to learn judgment and compassion
from the study of our past
—C.A.N.

Text copyright © 2004 by Susan Campbell Bartoletti
Illustrations copyright © 2004 by Claire A. Nivola

All rights reserved. For information about permission to reproduce selections from this book,
write to Permissions, Houghton Mifflin Company, 215 Park Avenue South, New York, New York 10003.

www.houghtonmifflinbooks.com

The text of this book is set in 14-point Bembo.
The illustrations are watercolor and gauche.

Library of Congress Cataloging-in-Publication Data is on file.

Printed in Singapore
TWP 10 9 8 7 6 5 4 3 2 1

It was 1812, and the United States was at war with Britain. A country at war needed plenty of flags.

In Baltimore, a twelve-year-old girl named Caroline Pickersgill and her mother, Mary, made flags.

Caroline and her mother sewed flags so that militia and cavalry officers could direct their men during battles on land.

They sewed flags so that navy ships could communicate with each other during battles at sea.

They sewed flags for the privateers that attacked British ships.

But no matter how many flags they made and no matter how many battles the Americans fought, the Americans could not defeat the British.

One summer day, Caroline and her mother welcomed three military officers to their flag shop. The men ordered an American flag for Fort McHenry, the fort guarding the waters near Baltimore.

"The flag must be so large that the British will have no trouble seeing it from a distance," said one officer.

Excited, Caroline and her mother set to work right away. Out of wool bunting, they cut pieces for broad red and white stripes.

They cut a large field of dark blue.

They cut white cotton stars.

Day after day, they sewed stitch after stitch, red stripe after white stripe, star after star.

Caroline's grandmother and cousins helped.

So did her mother's slave.

Her house servant, too.

Night after night, they worked by candlelight, long past bedtime.

The wool bunting itched.

The needle pricked.

Caroline's fingers ached, and her eyes felt gritty and sore.

But, inch by inch, they sewed until the flag spilled over their laps and lay in folds on the floor.

Soon the flag outgrew the sewing room. They carried it to a large malt house, where ale was made during the winter months.

They spread out the flag on the malt house floor.

And they sewed still more.

Finally, after six long weeks, the last star was sewn into place.

The last threads were snipped and knotted.

From hoist to fly, it was the largest flag Caroline had ever seen.

The flag was delivered to Fort McHenry, where soldiers raised it high
above the ramparts.

Each day Caroline looked for her flag as it waved over the fort.
It looked tiny in the distance, but she felt proud.

Over the next year, the flag shop grew even busier.
Caroline and her mother sewed more flags.
The Americans fought more battles.
Yet they could not defeat the British, once and for all.
And so a difficult year passed.

Early one August morning, a horse clattered down the Baltimore streets. "British sails!" its rider shouted. "In the Chesapeake Bay!"

Caroline knew British ships meant one thing—invasion!

All over Baltimore church bells clanged, calling militiamen to arms.

Men and boys shouldered long muskets and lined up on the parade grounds.

A snare drum rolled. A bugle flared. A commander shouted, "Forward, march!"

The militiamen tramped off to rout the British.

All that day, Caroline tried to go about her work.

She sewed.

She swept.

She looked for her flag and waited for news.

She swept and sewed and waited still more.

The next day, Caroline heard a low rumble like a distant thunderstorm.

Cannon.

She whispered a prayer for the men.

Later, terrible news was again shouted in the streets. The Americans had fought a battle and lost. Now British troops were headed to destroy Washington.

That night, men, women, and children spilled out onto rooftops. They watched the sky over Washington. It glowed an eerie orange. The British were burning the capital!

Caroline looked out across the dark harbor toward Fort McHenry. She couldn't see the flag, but she trusted it was there.

Baltimore prepared to defend itself.

Around the city, men dug trenches and built earthworks. Shovels scraped and clinked. Dirt flew.

Women and children carried biscuits and sweet tea to the volunteers.

In the channel near Fort McHenry, men sunk small ships and barges to block the harbor.

Women and children tore soft cloths into bandages.

Men moved gunboats into position, ready to fire on British ships.

Once more, Baltimore waited.

A day.

A week.

Two weeks.

The city held its breath.

And went to church.

And went to work.

And waited for the British to strike.

Early one September morning, a loud roar rocked the flag shop.

Caroline rushed to the window.

British ships were bombing Fort McHenry!

Fort McHenry's guns blazed back!

Hour after hour, bombs burst louder than thunder.

Hour after hour, rockets screamed and flashed brighter than lightning.

The shop trembled and shook. The streets turned thick with smoke.

The smell of burnt powder filled the air.

The British ships crept closer and closer.

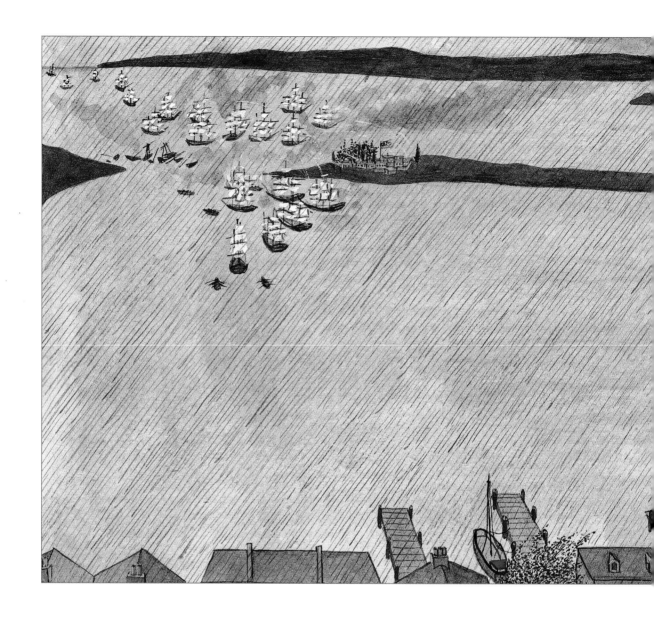

Evening came.

The sky darkened with storm.

Rain fell.

Soon thunder and lightning joined the cannon and rockets.

Ships and fort and sky boomed and flashed together.

Each time the sky lit up, Caroline saw that her flag was still there.

At midnight, the bombing stopped.

One minute.

Ten minutes.

An hour, and all was still.

Caroline longed for morning light.
Now she could only sit.
And hold on to courage.
She tried not to sleep.
But she did.

At dawn Caroline awoke. The rain had stopped. Everywhere, sky and water and land looked gray. She couldn't see the fort.

A breeze passed through the window. Slowly, the sky cleared.

There, hoisted high above the ramparts, Caroline saw a tired flag hanging from its staff in the damp morning air . . .

A wool bunting flag sewn full of broad stripes and bright stars.

With needles that pricked.

And fingers that ached.

A flag sewn full of pride and courage and hope.

Author's Note

On a visit to the Smithsonian Institution in Washington, D.C., I saw the Star-Spangled Banner, the very flag that had inspired Francis Scott Key to write the words that became the national anthem of the United States.

Awestruck, I wondered whose hands had sewn such an enormous flag. When I learned that a thirteen-year-old girl named Caroline Pickersgill had helped her mother, Mary, sew the flag, I wanted to tell their story.

Caroline Pickersgill was born in 1800 into a family of important flag makers. Her widowed grandmother, Rebecca Young, sewed flags for General George Washington's Continental Army during the Revolutionary War. After Caroline's father died, her mother opened the Baltimore shop in 1807.

In 1812, the United States declared war on Britain because Britain interfered with American overseas trade: British ships stopped American merchant ships, confiscated their cargoes, and forced American sailors to serve as crew on British ships. Though many Americans opposed the war, others wanted the young republic to assert its independence. Still others saw an opportunity for the United States to win parts of British Canada.

In June 1813, Major George Armistead commissioned Mary Pickersgill to sew the large garrison flag. "Which she did," wrote Caroline years later, "being an exceedingly patriotic woman. . . . My mother worked many nights until twelve o'clock to complete it. I assisted her."

Though Caroline doesn't say, it's likely that other people helped. The helpers may have included Caroline's grandmother, her two cousins, one free black woman who worked as a servant, and a slave woman owned by Mary. Today, it's ironic to think that a slave helped to sew a flag that represents freedom.

The attack on Fort McHenry took place September 13 and 14, 1814. We don't know for certain whether Caroline could see the flag from her house, but we do know that her neighbors watched the bombardment from their rooftops and nearby Federal Hill. Over a twenty-five-hour period, the British fired more than 1,500 bombs and 600 rockets.

An American lawyer, Francis Scott Key, watched the battle as he was detained on a British ship. Throughout the night, Key saw the "bombs bursting in air" and the "rockets' red glare." Filled with emotion, he jotted down words and phrases. Soon afterward, he turned the words and phrases into a poem, which later became the lyrics to our national anthem.

After the war, Major Armistead placed another order with Mary Pickersgill. "[He] declared that no one but the maker of the flag should mend it," said Caroline. And Mary did.

FLAG FACTS:

★ The Star-Spangled Banner has fifteen stripes and fifteen stars, even though there were eighteen states in 1812. In 1818, Congress mandated that the flag would have thirteen stripes to represent the thirteen original colonies and that a star would be added for each new state.

★ The eighty-pound flag measures thirty by forty-two feet. It contains about four hundred yards of bunting and an estimated 350,000 stitches. Each finished stripe measures two feet wide and is pieced together of varying lengths of material. The stars, two feet wide from point to point, are also pieced. Mary used a reverse appliqué method to sew the stars onto the blue field.

★ Mary was paid $405.90. At the time, it was considered a good wage for a woman.

★ Some historians question whether the garrison flag or a smaller storm flag (also sewn by Mary Pickersgill) flew over Fort McHenry during the bombardment. They point out that it was standard military practice to fly a storm flag during bad weather and enemy bombardment rather than risk damage to an expensive garrison flag. Other historians argue that the damage to the Star-Spangled Banner indicates that it was flown during the battle. They suggest that the enormous flag might have served as a helpful marker for the British.

★ Francis Scott Key's poem "The Defense of Fort McHenry" was originally sung to the popular British tune "Anacreon in Heaven." Soon the song became known as "The Star-Spangled Banner." In 1931, Congress officially recognized "The Star-Spangled Banner" as our national anthem.

★ Today the Star-Spangled Banner is displayed at the Smithsonian Institution, Washington, D.C. Caroline's home, the Star-Spangled Banner Flag House, is preserved as a National Historic Landmark in Baltimore, Maryland.

SOURCES CONSULTED BY THE AUTHOR:

Johnston, Sally, et al. *The Star-Spangled Banner Flag House.* Lawrenceburg, Indiana: Creative Company, 1999.

Lord, Walter. *The Dawn's Early Light.* New York: W. W. Norton, 1972.

Molotsky, Irwin. *The Flag, the Poet, and the Song: The Story of the Star-Spangled Banner.* New York: Dutton, 2001.

New York Evening Post, August to September 1814.

Pitch, Anthony S. *The Burning of Washington: The British Invasion of 1814.* Annapolis, Maryland: Naval Institute Press, 1998.

Purdy, Caroline Pickersgill. Letter to Georgiana Armistead Appleton, 1876. Appleton Family Papers, Massachusetts Historical Society, Boston.

———. Letter to Georgiana Armistead Appleton, undated. American Antiquarian Society, Worcester, Massachusetts.

Taylor, Lonn. *The Star-Spangled Banner: The Flag That Inspired the National Anthem.* New York: Harry N. Abrams, 2000.

★   ★   ★

Acknowledgments: The author and illustrator thank Peter Drummey (Massachusetts Historical Society, Boston), Sally Johnston (The Star-Spangled Banner Flag House and 1812 Museum, Baltimore, Maryland), Thomas Knoles (American Antiquarian Society, Worcester, Massachusetts), Scott Sheads (Fort McHenry National Monument and Historic Site), Clare Sheridan (American Textile Museum, Lowell, Massachusetts) Lonn Taylor (National Museum of American History, Smithsonian Institution, Washington, D.C.), and folks at the Maryland Historical Society (Baltimore).